HOW TO INTERPRET YOUR DREAMS

ANTHONY EKANEM

ISBN 979-888521398-1

Dedicated to my family and the readers.

Contents

Contents

Foreword

"Last night, I had the strangest dream!" How many conversations in your life have started that way? People are fascinated with the movies that play in their heads while they're sleeping. Some believe that dreams can predict the future. Others say that dreams depict real life. Still, others believe that dreams are a manifestation of what we want to be. Interpreting dreams has evolved over the years to what some consider an art form.

Consider some of these other facts about dreams and dreaming:

- Everybody dreams. Simply because you do not remember your dream does not mean that you did not dream.

- Dreams are indispensable. A lack of dream activity can mean protein deficiency or a personality disorder.

- Men tend to dream more about other men, while women dream equally about men and women.

- People who are giving up smoking have longer and more intense dreams.

- Toddlers do not dream about themselves. They do not appear in their dreams until the age of three or four.

- If you are snoring, then you cannot be dreaming.

- Blind people do dream. Whether visual images will

appear in their dream depends on whether they were blind at birth or became blind later in life. But vision is not the only sense that constitutes a dream. Sounds, tactility, and smell become hypersensitive for the blind and their dreams are based on these senses.

The dream world is fascinating, full of speculation, hope, and sometimes even fear. We can wake up from a good dream feeling refreshed and hopeful. On the other hand, we can wake up from a bad dream feeling tense and apprehensive.

Ever since Freud's *Interpretation of Dreams*was published, there has been recognition of the importance of dreams. But even before that, there were dream interpretations. People had superstitious notions about dreams - for example, "Something is going to happen because I dreamed it was going to happen."

This is a common misconception. Regardless of what some people might say, if you dream you are falling and don't wake up before you hit the ground in your dream, you will not die. If you dream that someone close to you dies, that's not an omen to warn you of their death. Dreams do not predict the future.

What dreams can do is provide a sense of insight into ourselves. They can help us cope with situations we're unsure about. They can guide us in a certain direction when faced with uncertainty. They can simply give us an overall good feeling as we dream of something pleasant.

The dream state is an experimental playground that gives you a chance to explore and express emotions without the usual inhibitions you may display in your waking life. Dreams provide an avenue of expression for that part of yourself that knows both your history and your potential as a spiritual being.

They are another way the universe provides guidance about relationships, careers, and health problems. Through dreams, you may find answers to your spiritual questions and even receive encouragement to some challenge in your life. While some dreams may allow you to release bottled emotions from your day's activities, others can lead to profound insights psychologically or spiritually.

Acquiring the ability to interpret your dreams is a powerful tool. In analyzing your dreams, you can learn about your deep secrets and hidden feelings. No one is a better expert at interpreting your dreams than yourself.

In this book, we'll look at dreams and dreaming as a science as well as the various meanings that dream content can have. This is not meant to be a definitive guide to dreams. It is simply a starting point for you to look at what "movies" your subconscious is creating at night and how you can apply it to your life and effect change if needed.

Remember that a dream unifies the body, mind, and spirit. It provides you with insight into yourself and a means for self-exploration. In understanding your dreams, you will have a better understanding and discovery of your true self. So, stay a while - explore, discover, have fun, and find out what's in your dreams!

Preface

"Last night, I had the strangest dream!" How many conversations in your life have started that way? People are fascinated with the movies that play in their heads while they're sleeping. Some believe that dreams can predict the future. Others say that dreams depict real life. Still, others believe that dreams are a manifestation of what we want to be. Interpreting dreams has evolved over the years to what some consider an art form.

Consider some of these other facts about dreams and dreaming:

- Everybody dreams. Simply because you do not remember your dream does not mean that you did not dream.
- Dreams are indispensable. A lack of dream activity can mean protein deficiency or a personality disorder.
- Men tend to dream more about other men, while women dream equally about men and women.
- People who are giving up smoking have longer and more intense dreams.
- Toddlers do not dream about themselves. They do not appear in their dreams until the age of three or four.
- If you are snoring, then you cannot be dreaming.
- Blind people do dream. Whether visual images will

appear in their dream depends on whether they were blind at birth or became blind later in life. But vision is not the only sense that constitutes a dream. Sounds, tactility, and smell become hypersensitive for the blind and their dreams are based on these senses.

The dream world is fascinating, full of speculation, hope, and sometimes even fear. We can wake up from a good dream feeling refreshed and hopeful. On the other hand, we can wake up from a bad dream feeling tense and apprehensive.

Ever since Freud's *Interpretation of Dreams* was published, there has been recognition of the importance of dreams. But even before that, there were dream interpretations. People had superstitious notions about dreams - for example, "Something is going to happen because I dreamed it was going to happen."

This is a common misconception. Regardless of what some people might say, if you dream you are falling and don't wake up before you hit the ground in your dream, you will not die. If you dream that someone close to you dies, that's not an omen to warn you of their death. Dreams do not predict the future.

What dreams can do is provide a sense of insight into ourselves. They can help us cope with situations we're unsure about. They can guide us in a certain direction when faced with uncertainty. They can simply give us an overall good feeling as we dream of something pleasant.

The dream state is an experimental playground that gives you a chance to explore and express emotions without the usual inhibitions you may display in your waking life. Dreams provide an avenue of expression for that part of yourself that knows both your history and your potential as a spiritual being.

They are another way the universe provides guidance about relationships, careers, and health problems. Through dreams, you may find answers to your spiritual questions and even receive encouragement to some challenge in your life. While some dreams may allow you to release bottled emotions from your day's activities, others can lead to profound insights psychologically or spiritually.

Acquiring the ability to interpret your dreams is a powerful tool. In analyzing your dreams, you can learn about your deep secrets and hidden feelings. No one is a better expert at interpreting your dreams than yourself.

In this book, we'll look at dreams and dreaming as a science as well as the various meanings that dream content can have. This is not meant to be a definitive guide to dreams. It is simply a starting point for you to look at what "movies" your subconscious is creating at night and how you can apply it to your life and effect change if needed.

Remember that a dream unifies the body, mind, and spirit. It provides you with insight into yourself and a means for self-exploration. In understanding your dreams, you will have a better understanding and discovery of your true self. So, stay a while - explore, discover, have fun, and find out what's in your dreams!

Acknowledgements

I hereby acknowledge all who inspired the writing of this book.

CHAPTER ONE

Did We Always Dream?

That may seem like a silly question, but think about early man. Have people always dreamt even when the world around them was quite simple and mundane? The answer is yes. What did the man do with these odd images that appeared during their sleep? Well, they did what we do today – tried to interpret them!

Dream interpretations date back to 3000 - 4000 B.C. where they were documented on clay tablets. For as long as we have been able to communicate our dreams, we have been fascinated with them and strive to understand them.

People in primal societies were unable to distinguish between the dream world and reality. They not only saw the dream world as an extension of reality, but that the dream realm was a more powerful world.

Back in the Greek and Roman era, dreams were often seen in a religious context and messages from the gods. Temples were built around the power of dreams. It was believed that sick people who slept in these temples would be sent cures through their dreams.

In Egypt, priests also acted as dream interpreters. The Egyptians recorded their dreams in hieroglyphics. People with vivid and significant dreams were believed to be blessed and were considered special. People who had the power to interpret dreams were looked up to and seen as divinely gifted. In the Bible, there are over seven hundred mentions of dreams.

Tracing back to those ancient cultures, people had always been inclined to interpret dreams. Dreams were also seen as prophetic and an omen from outside spirits. People often looked to their dreams for signs of warning and advice from a deity, from the dead or even the works of a demon. Sometimes they look to their dreams for what to do or what course of action to take.

Dreams often dictated the actions of political and military leaders. In fact, in the Green and Roman era, dream interpreters even accompanied military leaders into battle to help. Some interpreters aided the medicine men in a diagnosis. Dreams offered a vital clue for healers in finding what was wrong with the dreamer.

Dreaming can be seen as an actual place that your spirit and soul leaves every night to go and visit. The Chinese believed that the soul leaves the body to go into this world. However, if they should be suddenly awakened, their soul may fail to return to the body. For this reason, some Chinese today, are wary of alarm clocks.

Some Native American tribes and Mexican civilizations share this same notion of a distinct dream dimension. They believed that their ancestors lived in their dreams and take on non-human forms like plants. They see those dreams as a way of visiting and having contact with their ancestors. Dreams also helped to point to their mission or role in life.

During the Middle Ages, dreams were seen as evil, and their images were temptations from the devil. In the vulnerable sleep state, the devil was believed to fill the mind of humans with poisonous thoughts. He did his dirty work through dreams attempting to mislead humans down a wrong path.

The potential for an immense array of experiences in consciousness is always there. What we receive depends upon our attitudes, motivations, the measure of our attunement, and the extent to which we have made applicable what was received in earlier dreams and in waking experiences.

The dream world is a strange yet fascinating place! There are several different kinds of dreams. Let's look at those in our next section.

CHAPTER TWO

Types of Dreams

Daydreams

Studies have shown that we all have the tendency to daydream an average of 70-120 minutes a day. Day dreaming is classified as a level of consciousness between sleep and wakefulness. It occurs during our waking hours when we let our imagination carry us away. As our minds begin to wander and our level of awareness decreases, we lose ourselves in our imagined scenario and fantasy.

Lucid Dreams

Lucid dreams occur when you realize you are dreaming. "Wait a second. This is only a dream!" Most dreamers wake themselves up once they realize that they are only dreaming. Other dreamers have cultivated the skill to remain in the lucid state of dreaming. They become an active participant in their dreams, making decisions in their dreams and influencing the dream's outcome without awakening.

Nightmares

A nightmare is a disturbing dream that causes the dreamer to wake up feeling anxious and frightened. Nightmares may be a response to real-life trauma and situations. This type of nightmare falls under a special category called Post-traumatic Stress Nightmare (PSN).

Nightmares may also occur because we have ignored or refused to accept a particular life situation. Research shows that most people who have regular nightmares have had a family history of psychiatric problems, bad drug experiences, people who have contemplated suicide, or rocky relationships. Nightmares are an indication of a fear that needs to be acknowledged and confronted. We'll have more later in the book about nightmares and steps you can take to overcome them.

Recurring Dreams

Recurring dreams repeat themselves with little variation in the story or theme. These dreams may be positive, but most often they are nightmarish in content. Dreams may recur because a conflict depicted in the dream remains unresolved or ignored. Once you have found a resolution to the problem, your recurring dreams will cease.

Healing Dreams

Healing dreams serve as messages for the dreamer in regards to their health. Many dream experts believe that dreams can help us avoid potential health problems and help us to heal when we are ill. Our bodies can communicate to us through our dreams to "tell" us that something is not quite right with our bodies even before any physical symptoms show up. Dreams of this nature may be telling the dreamer that he or she needs to go to the dentist or doctor.

Prophetic Dreams

Prophetic dreams also referred to as precognitive or psychic dreams are dreams that seemingly foretell the future. One rational theory to explain this phenomenon is that our dreaming mind can piece together bits of information and observation that we normally overlook or that we do not seriously consider. In other words, our unconscious mind knows what is coming before we consciously piece together the same information

Signal Dreams

Signal dreams help you know how to solve problems or make decisions in your waking life.

Epic Dreams

Epic dreams (or Great dreams) are so huge, so compelling, and so vivid that you cannot ignore them. The details of such dreams remain with you for years, as if you dreamt it last night. These dreams possess much beauty and contain much archetypal symbology. When you wake up from such a dream, you feel that you have discovered something profound or amazing about yourself or the world. It feels like a life-changing experience

You might be wondering what exactly is going on in your head when you dream.

CHAPTER THREE

Why Do We Dream?

The brain receives stimuli from many different sources all day long. There are far too many stimuli for it to process. The mind prioritizes the stimuli and makes you aware of those that need immediate attention (the crying baby, the out-of-control car, your boss' request) so that you may act accordingly.

The stimuli that you are not consciously aware of are nevertheless noted by the brain, but on a subconscious level (the drip of the bathroom water faucet, the remark by a coworker at the water cooler while you were on the telephone.)

Furthermore, you feel emotions all day. Some you acknowledge and act on (you say thank you and smile when you are complimented.) Some you repress or do not allow yourself to act on (you don't punch your boss in the nose when he tells you the report you worked on for a week is no longer needed.)

Traumatic experiences occur that you face (you call the police) or if it is too painful, you deny them happening and send them deep into your subconscious (repression).

In addition to all these emotions and stimuli the brain must process daily, it also keeps your body functioning; it remembers names and faces; it allows you to talk and walk and chew gum (sometimes all at the same time), and performs numerous other activities that you take for granted.

You must admit - that's a lot to do. At night, when your body must rest, the mind continues working. When no longer called upon to type letters and do the grocery shopping, the brain concentrates on processing all those subconscious stimuli and emotions (while still maintaining body temperature and breathing, etc.)

This is why we dream. Only you are not awake to receive the signals at a conscious level - you cannot hear or see or touch (at a conscious level) while you are sleeping. The brain must resort to other means to get the signals through to your conscious mind. This is why we dream the way we do.

The mind uses everything at its disposal (which is everything it has ever been exposed to) to get the message across. Simply put, dreaming is the minds way of processing all the stimuli and emotions it has received during the day or repressed over time, so that you may act on them.

All in all, it's a neat system. But unless you are remembering and making sense of your dreams, you are missing out on countless opportunities to learn about yourself and experience life to its fullest.

Even though we've addressed it before, it bears repeating. Why should you try and remember your dreams?

CHAPTER FOUR

Why Remember Your Dreams?

Your dreaming mind has access to information that is not readily available to you when you are awake. Your dreams may reveal your secret desires and subconscious feelings. In remembering your dreams, you will have increased knowledge about yourself, bringing about self-awareness and self-healing. Dreams are an extension of how you perceive yourself. They can be a source of inspiration, wisdom, and joy.

You don't have to interpret your dreams to solve your problems. But just as there is the saying that "Death cures cigarette smoking," you might find that listening to your dreams may help you solve your problems before you run out of time.

Dreams are always "true"— it's just that what they mean isn't always what we think they mean. Sometimes a dream gives a warning of danger, but if you pay attention to the dream and change your ways the danger won't necessarily happen. And most often a dream's meaning will be metaphorical, not literal.

For example, a woman may dream that her husband is having a sexual affair, but it would be a mistake to conclude that her husband is having an affair. The dream is simply providing the woman with graphic evidence that she somehow feels betrayed by her husband. Once she acknowledges that feeling, she can then start examining her life consciously—and honestly—to find out why she feels betrayed and what she needs to do about it.

All dreams essentially tell us one important thing: "Wake up!" That is, just as you must wake up from a dream to remember it, the dream itself is telling you to "wake up" to the truth that you try to hide from others—and yourself. Of course, there is a positive as well as a negative side to remembering and interpreting your dreams.

The negative side is that you may come across a side of yourself that you don't like or are afraid to know about. You may discover that you aren't (always) the "Miss Goody Two Shoes" or "Mr Nice Guy" that you profess to be during the day. You may discover that your childhood was not all ice cream, roller-skating and amusement parks. You may end up shedding light on dark places and recall secrets long repressed. This can be scary stuff.

The positive side is that you go through a metamorphosis or catharsis and become -- you. You become the "you" that you were always meant to be. You will become truer to yourself and therefore, you will find that you are happier.

Learning to recall your dreams may help you become a more assertive, creative person. In remembering your dreams, you are expressing and confronting your feelings. Remembering your dreams can help you come to terms with stressful aspects of your lives.

But this may be easier said than done. Five minutes after the end of the dream, half the content is forgotten. After ten minutes, 90% is lost. Dreamers, who are awakened right after sleep, can recall their dreams more vividly than those who slept through the night until morning. Remembering your dreams is vital to interpreting them. So, how can you better remember your dreams?

How to Remember Your Dreams

When beginning the steps towards interpreting your dreams, many people find it helpful to keep a notebook – a dream journal, if you will – right next to your bed with a pen or pencil. As soon as you are physically able, begin your journal.

Write down your dream as soon as you remember it. Write down everything you remember, even if it doesn't make sense. Most often, the parts that don't make sense or are out of place are the most valuable. Every detail, even the minutest element in your dream is important and must be considered when analyzing your dreams. Look closely at the characters, animals, objects, places, emotions, and even colours and numbers that are depicted in your dreams.

Ask yourself, "What does this remind me of?" Write down the first thing that comes to your mind. This will likely be the real situation in your life that is symbolized in the dream. What did that real-life situation make you feel like? If this is the same feeling represented in your dream, you're on the right track. Often when there is more than one part to your dream (more than one storyline) that usually means there are two things your subconscious is trying to tell you.

Remember that we have between four and seven dreams per night. If you wake up from a dream, write it down. Don't roll over and go back to sleep. If you don't write it down, you'll never remember it in the morning! At the very least, you can jot down the basic premise of the dream and go back in the morning to fill in the rest of the details such as feelings, etc.

Suggest to yourself every night as you fall asleep, "I will remember my dreams." Say this over and over. Your subconscious will act on this subtle suggestion. Practice keen observation in your dreams through self-suggestion before sleep. When a problem confronts you, you might want to ask by prayer for guidance to be sent to you through your dreams.

Trust your instincts! If something seems important, it probably is. Try not to let your logical side take over. So, you've got your dreams down on paper. Where do you go next? The next step would be interpretation.

CHAPTER FIVE

Interpreting Your Dreams

Interpreting your dreams can be a lot of fun. As we've said, it can also give you valuable insight. Dreams are like coded messages from your unconscious mind. When you decode them, you gain access to a wealth of intuitive wisdom.

Remember that only you can interpret your dreams. Many people have published "Dream Dictionaries" that describe what each part of the dream symbolizes. The same dream can have infinite meanings, depending on the person who dreamed it. The important thing is, what does it mean to YOU?

Interpreting dreams isn't something you can pick up and become an expert at right away. It takes time and practice. First, keep the following things in mind:

1. Dreams are the reaction of the inner self to daytime activity and often show the way out of the dilemma. So, relate them to current activity because dreams may be retrospective as well as prospective.
2. Observe recurrent dreams, as well as the serially progressive ones. These often illustrate progress or failure. Be practical in your interpretations. Always look

first for a lesson. What have you refused to face or been ignoring?

3. Dreams come to guide and help, not to amuse. They direct your attention to errors of omission and commission and offer encouragement for the right endeavours. They also give us the opportunity to pray for others and to help them bear their burdens.
4. Look for past-life experiences in your dreams. These manifest themselves not only in colour but in the proper costume and setting of their period. They come to warn you against repeating the same old mistakes; to explain your relationship and reactions to certain people and places; to reduce your confusion; to enable you to better understand life. Dreams that are unchanged through the years indicate the dreamer's resistance to change.

The difficulty most people have with interpreting their dreams is that they aren't objective enough. Their familiarity with the people and places in their dreams obscures the dreams meaning. Experts have come up with the "I AM and I NEED" formula, devised to overcome this. Here's how it works.

Once you have your dream written on paper, get two different coloured pens. Using one colour, underline every negative word or phrase in the dream which indicates limitation, disrespect, containment, avoidance, or damage.

Using the other colour, underline every positive word or phrase. You now make two lists. List the negative words and phrases under a column titled I AM. List the positive words and phrases under a column titled I NEED. You are almost ready to interpret your dream. Determine the subject matter of the dream. The location where the dream takes place is one of the best methods for doing this. When you have determined the subject matter take each of the phrases or words in the 'I AM' column and fit them into the following sentence.

When it comes to my (subject matter) I AM (phrase or keyword)

Change the phrase or keyword slightly to force the sentence to make sense. If you cannot determine the subject matter apply the keywords to yourself in general. This exercise tells you how you feel or react to the subject matter of the dream. When you have done this read through the 'I NEED' column to learn what you must do to correct the problem. To get the meaning put each of the phrases or keywords into the sentence,

When it comes to my (subject matter) I NEED (phrase or keyword)

Let's take an example. Using the sentence 'The dead woman lay on the cold hard slab'. The negative keywords are: dead, cold, and hard. Women, in dreams, can represent emotions so in this case, the sentences constructed would be:

- When it comes to my emotions, I am dead.
- When it comes to my emotions, I am cold.
- When it comes to my emotions, I am hard.

The meaning is obvious. By analyzing just one sentence from a dream we have learned a lot about the dreamer. Using this technique, you now have all the information you need to start interpreting your dreams. However, it takes practice to be able to apply what you have learned. Be patient with your efforts.

Not all dream interpretations will be cut and dried, but it is a way to remain objective when you are analyzing what your dreams mean and how best to put the messages they are conveying to good use in your life. Keep in mind that most dreams are NOT precognitive, and once one learns the subtle differences between a precognitive dream versus a regular dream, they are easily discernable and will put your mind at ease.

The first thing everyone should consider is the typical universal symbology of the dream images. For instance, death symbolizes the end of something ready for change, and a new beginning. Most people start highly resistive to changes of any sort and see any upcoming change in their life as something foreboding and scary. Death dreams are usually about change.

The symbols and what they represent is the most fascinating part of dream interpretation. There are hundreds of them. We don't have the space to address ALL of them, but we will touch on some of the most recurring themes in dreams as well as the symbols of those dreams and what they mean.

Most Common Dream Images

One very important thing to keep in mind is to interpret symbols within the context of the dream they appear in, rather than piece by piece which would leave too much room for error. There are thousands of symbols, and it depends upon the context of one's dream as to what they all mean for him or her.

Look at it this way...a dream is like a puzzle, and although several pieces are quickly pieced together because they are so obvious, the puzzle isn't complete until all the pieces are placed together bit by bit. Then you have the complete picture; until then, you'll only have disjointed images that don't add up to anything coherent, and you'll still be confused. Remember that and try not to piecemeal a dream; it needs to be fully interpreted or it will most likely be wrong. Let's look at some of the more common dream images and what they could mean.

Teeth Falling Out

This is probably the most prevalent dream image that people report. It is disturbing to them because it affects vanity and personal appearance – but only in the dream! a dream about one's teeth falling out usually symbolizes that the dreamer is having a challenge getting their voice heard, or feelings acknowledged.

This may be referring to their conversations with a particular person such as their significant other, boss, or friend; or can be generalized for shy people, to include almost everyone they meet.

The dreamer needs to brush up on conversational skills, believe in the value of their own opinion, and learn how to be less intimidated by aggressive people, and become more assertive and make their voice heard. Once they do that, this dream (which is a common recurring dream) should evolve and show improvement or disappear altogether.

Another theory is that dreams about your teeth reflect your anxiety about your appearance and how others perceive you. Sadly, we live in a world where good looks are valued highly and your teeth play an important role in conveying that image. Teeth are used in the game of flirtations, whether it is a dazzling and gleaming smile or affectionate necking. These dreams may stem from a fear of your sexual impotence or the consequences of getting old. Teeth are an important feature of our attractiveness and presentation to others. Everybody worries about how they appear to others. Caring about our appearance is natural and healthy.

There are cultural interpretations of this type of dream as well. A scriptural interpretation for bad or falling teeth indicates that you are putting your faith, trust, and beliefs in what man thinks rather than in the word of God. The bible says that God speaks once, yea twice in a dream or a vision to hide pride from us, to keep us back from the pit, to open our ears (spiritually) and to instruct and correct us.

In the Greek culture, when you dream about loose, rotten, or missing teeth, it indicates that a family member or close friend is very sick or even near death.

According to the Chinese, there is a saying that your teeth will fall out if you are telling lies. It has also been said that if you dream of your teeth falling out, then it symbolizes money. This is based on the old tooth fairy story. If you lose a tooth and leave it under the pillow, a tooth fairy would bring you money.

Flying

Dreams about flying usually represent freedom from the physical body, as we experience in sleep and while dreaming where we don't use our physical bodies but instead use our mental and spiritual bodies to experience our dreams. It's one of the first things people attempt to do when they gain control of their dreams and start lucid dreaming.

Everybody seems to have a natural inclination to want to fly unless that is changed by a fear of flying due to a frightening incident in their waking lives. Flying = freedom; either a desire for freedom, an "escape" from restraints in your physical life (like a mini-vacation for the mind) or any number of possibilities.

Tie it in with the context of your dream...what were you doing in your dream besides flying? How did it make you feel? Also, the type of flying here is the person flying on their own without an aeroplane or any aircraft at all. That would be a different symbol dealing with spiritual awareness, among other things. Flying dreams fall under a category of dreams where you become aware that you are dreaming, known as lucid dreaming. Many dreamers have described the ability to fly in their dreams as an exhilarating, joyful, and liberating experience.

If you are flying with ease and enjoying the scene and landscape below, then it suggests that you are on top of a situation. You have risen above something. It may also mean that you have gained a different perspective on things. Flying dreams and the ability to control your flight is representative of your sense of power.

Having difficulties staying in flight indicates a lack of power in controlling your circumstances. You may be struggling to stay aloft and stay on course. Things like power lines, trees, or mountains may further obstruct your flight. These barriers represent a particular obstacle or person who is standing in your way in your waking life. You need to identify who or what is hindering you from moving forward.

If you are feeling fear when you are flying or that you feel that you are flying too high, then it suggests that you are afraid of challenges and success. In reality, we cannot fly. Thus, such dreams may represent that which is beyond our physical limitations. In your mind, you can be anybody and do anything. Another way of interpreting flying dreams is that these dreams symbolize your strong mind and will. You feel undefeatable and nobody can tell you what you cannot do and accomplish. Undoubtedly these dreams leave you a great sense of freedom.

Being Caught in a Tornado

This symbol points to emotional turmoil, as in a "whirlwind of emotions"; or rapid or sudden changes in your life. It is a sign to "get a grip" on what is possibly spinning out of control & deal more effectively with your emotions. Meditation and finding some private "think time" for yourself would be a good idea.

Being Naked

Dreaming that you are completely or partially naked is very common. Nudity symbolizes a variety of things depending on your real-life situation. Becoming mortified at the realization that you are walking around naked in public is often a reflection of your vulnerability or shamefulness. You may be hiding something and are afraid that others can nevertheless see right through you. Metaphorically clothes are a means of concealment. With clothes, you can hide your identity or be someone else. But without them, everything is hanging out for all to see. You are left without any defences.

The dream may be telling you that you are trying to be something that you are not. Or that you are fearful of being ridiculed and disgraced. If you are in a new relationship, you may have some fears or apprehension in revealing your true feelings.

Nudity also symbolizes being caught off guard. Finding yourself naked at work or in a classroom, suggests that you are unprepared for a project at work or school. You may be uninformed in making a well-formed decision. With all eyes on you, you have this fear of having some deed brought to public attention. You fear that people will see through your true self and you will be exposed as a fraud or a phoney.

Many times, when you realize that you are naked in your dream, no one else seems to notice. Everyone else in the dream is going about their business without giving a second look at your nakedness. This implies that your fears are unfounded; no one will notice except you. You may be magnifying the situation and making an issue of nothing. On the other hand, such dreams may mean your desire (or failure) to get noticed.

For a small percentage of you, dreaming that you are proud of your nakedness and show no embarrassment or shame, then it symbolizes your unrestricted freedom. You have nothing to hide and are proud of who you are. The dream is about a new sense of honesty, openness, and carefree nature.

Being Chased

Chase dreams often stem from feelings of anxiety in your walking life. The way we respond to anxiety and pressure in real life is typically manifested as a chase dream. Running is an instinctive response to physical threats in our environment.

Often in these dream scenarios, you are being pursued by some attacker, who wants to hurt or possibly kill you. You are running away, hiding, or trying to outwit your pursuer.

Chase dreams may represent your way of coping with fears, stress, or various situations in your waking life.

Instead of confronting the situation, you are running away and avoiding it. Ask yourself who is the one chasing you and you may gain some understanding and insight on the source of your fears and pressure.

The pursuer or attacker who is chasing you in your dream may also represent a part of yourself. Your feelings of anger, jealousy, fear, and possibly love, can assume the appearance of a threatening figure. You may be projecting these feelings onto the unknown chaser. Next time you have a chase dream, turn around and confront your pursuer. Ask them why they are chasing you.

One may be consumed by anger, jealousy, love, or self-destructive behaviour. For example, you may be drinking too much or exhibiting open hostility toward others around you. You may subconsciously be threatened by these actions which have been jeopardizing your relationships or career. Your dreams are a way of calling attention to these self-destructive actions.

More direct analysis of chase dreams is the fear of being attacked. Such dreams are more common among women than men, who may feel physically vulnerable in the urban environment. These dreams are inspired by fears of violence and sexual assault in which we are so over-exposed from the media. The violence that the media portrays magnifies our fears and how at-risk we all are.

Falling

Falling dreams are another theme that is quite common in the world of dreams. As we said earlier, contrary to a popular myth, you will not die if you do not wake up before your hit the ground during a fall.

As with most common dream themes, falling is an indication of insecurities, instabilities, and anxieties. You are feeling overwhelmed and out of control in some situations in your waking life. This may reflect the way you feel in your relationship or your work environment. You have lost your foothold and cannot hang on or keep up with the hustle and bustle of daily life. When you fall, there is nothing that you can hold on to. You are forced toward this downward motion without any control. This loss of control may parallel a waking situation in your life.

Falling dreams also often reflect a sense of failure or inferiority in some circumstance or situation. It may be the fear of failing in your job or school, loss of status, or failure in love. You feel shameful and lack a sense of pride. You are unable to keep up with the status quo or that you don't measure up. According to Freudian theory, dreams of falling indicate that you are contemplating giving into a sexual urge or impulse. You may be lacking indiscretion.

Falling dreams typically occur during the first stage of sleep. Dreams in this stage are often accompanied by muscle spasms of the arms, legs, and the whole body. Sometimes when we have these falling dreams, we feel our whole body jerk or twitch and we awaken from this jerk. It is thought that this jerking action is part of an arousal mechanism that allows the sleeper to awaken and become quickly alert and responsive to possible threats in the environment.

According to biblical interpretations, dreams about falling have a negative overtone and suggest that man is acting and walking according to his way of thinking and not those of the Lord.

Taking an Exam or Test

To dream that you are taking an exam indicates that you are being put to the test or being scrutinized in some way. Such dreams highlight your feelings of being anxious and agitated. You may find that you cannot answer any of the questions on the test or that the test is in some foreign language.

Is time running out and you find that you cannot complete the exam in the allowed time? Or are you late for the exam? Does your pencil keep breaking during the exam? Such factors contribute to you failing this test.

These dreams usually have to do with your self-esteem and confidence or your lack of. You are worried that you are not making the grade and measuring up to other people's expectations of you. You may also experience the fear of not being accepted, not being prepared, or not being good enough. You feel nervous, insecure and tend to believe the worst about yourself. These dreams also suggest that you may feel unprepared for a challenge. Rarely, are these dreams about the content of the test, but rather the process and how you are feeling during the examination-taking process. Generally, you feel distressed and frustrated. These feelings may parallel how you are feeling in a particular challenge or situation in your waking life.

Dreams of this nature are also an indication that you are being judged and this dream is a signal for you to examine an aspect of yourself that you may have been neglecting and need to pay attention to. You may harbour some guilt because of your neglect in preparation for a school exam, meeting, business project, or some challenge. Most of the time people who have such dreams are unlikely to fail a test in real life. This dream goes back to their fear and anxiety that they may not meet others‘ standards of them. They are afraid to let others down.

Now let's look at some specific symbols that appear in dreams and what they might mean.

DREAM SYMBOLS

Animals

To see animals in your dream represents your physical characteristic, primitive desires, and sexual nature, depending on the qualities of the animal. Animals symbolize the untamed and uncivilized aspects of who you are. Thus, to dream that you are fighting with an animal signifies a hidden part of yourself that you are trying to reject and push back into your subconscious. Refer to the specific animal in your dream.

To dream that animals can talk represents superior knowledge. Its message is often some form of wisdom. Alternatively, a talking animal denotes your potential to be all that you can be.

To dream that you are saving the life of an animal suggests that you are successfully acknowledging certain emotions and characteristics represented by the animal. The dream may also stem from feelings of inadequacy or being overwhelmed.

To see lab animals in your dream suggests that an aspect of yourself is being repressed. You feel that you are not able to fully express your desires and emotions. Alternatively, it suggests that you need to experiment with your fears, choices, and beliefs. Try not to limit yourself.

People

Every person that appears in a dream is supposed to represent an aspect of oneself, and not be about that other person at all; rather, it is a quality or characteristic about that person that your dream is focusing on, and how it applies to YOU.

Try to think about what aspect(s) this could be. It can be something you admire and wish to emulate and incorporate into your personality, or it could be a more negative characteristic that you may dislike intensely in your waking life, but which is telling you something about yourself and your beliefs, judgments, and attitude.

It could be a call to alter your thinking in some manner, to be more open-minded and accepting of this aspect in your personality because it is hampering your spiritual growth and making life harder for yourself.

The other person in your dream is always mirroring something back to you about YOURSELF. Try to discover what that something is and go from there. Once you get it through your head that the other person's appearance in your dream is NOT about them, but about YOU, then you will get much more successful interpreting your dreams. This takes constant reinforcement - I still find myself wanting to think it's about that other person instead of me. The only exception I know of is if the dream is precognitive.

Babies or Pregnancy

To dream that you are pregnant symbolizes an aspect of yourself or some aspect of your personal life that is growing and developing. You may not be ready to talk about it or act on it. This may also represent the birth of a new idea, direction, project, or goal.

To dream that you are pregnant with the baby dying inside of you suggests that a project you had put a lot of effort into is falling apart and slowly deteriorating. Nothing works out the way you want it to. If you are pregnant and having this dream, then it represents your anxieties about the pregnancy. In the first trimester, your dreams usually consist of tiny creatures, fuzzy animals, flowers, fruit, and water.

In the second trimester, your dreams will reflect your anxiety about being a good mother and concerns about possible complications with the birth. Dreams of giving birth to a non-human baby are also common during this period of pregnancy. Finally, in the third trimester, you will tend to dream about your mother.

For a man to dream that he got a girl pregnant, forewarns that his indiscriminate sexual activities may come back to haunt him. To see a baby in your dream signifies innocence, warmth, and new beginnings.

Babies may symbolize something in your inner nature, which is pure, vulnerable, and/or uncorrupted. Babies may represent an aspect of yourself that is vulnerable and helpless. If you dream that you forgot you had a baby, then it suggests that you are trying to hide your vulnerabilities; you do not want to let others know of your weaknesses.

If you dream that you are on your way to the hospital to have a baby, then it signifies your issues of dependency and your desire to be completely cared for. Perhaps you are trying to get out of some responsibility. If you are pregnant, then a more direct interpretation may simply mean that you are experiencing some anxieties about making it to the hospital when the time comes.

To dream of a crying baby, is indicative of a part of yourself that is deprived of attention and needs some nurturing. Alternatively, it represents your unfulfilled goals and a sense of lacking in your life.

To dream about a starving baby represents your dependence on others. You are experiencing some deficiency in your life that needs immediate attention and gratification.

To dream of an extremely small baby, symbolizes your helplessness and your fears of letting others become aware of your vulnerabilities and incompetence. You may be afraid to ask for help and as a result, tend to take matters into your own hands.

To see a dead baby in your dream symbolizes the ending of something that is part of you.

To dream that you are dipping a baby in and out of the water signifies regression. You are regressing to a time where you had no worries and responsibilities. Alternatively, it is reminiscent of when the baby is in the fetus and its comfort zone. Some expectant mothers even give birth in a pool, because the environment in the water mimics the environment in the uterus. It is less traumatic for the baby as it emerges into the world. So perhaps the dream is your search for your comfort zone.

Sex

To dream about sex refers to the psychological completion and the integration of contrasting aspects of the Self. You need to be more receptive and incorporate aspects of your dream sex partner into your character. Alternatively, and a more direct interpretation of the dream may be your libido's way of telling you that it's been too long since you have had sex. It may indicate repressed sexual desires and your needs for physical and emotional love.

To dream about sex with someone other than your spouse or significant other suggests dissatisfaction with the physical side of your relationship. On the other hand, it may be a harmless fantasy. In such situations, you may find that you are less inhibited sexually and you can even bring that sense of adventure to your existing relationship.

To dream that you are having sex with an ex or someone who is not your current mate, denotes your reservations about embarking on a new relationship or situation. You may feel nervous about exposing yourself or currently feel a resurgence of those old emotions and feelings that you felt back when you and your ex were together.

Believe it or not, it is not uncommon for people approaching their wedding to experience especially erotic adventures with partners other than their intended spouses. This may be due to the intensity of your sexual passion with your fiancé. It also relates to the new roles that you will be taking on and the uncertainty that that may bring.

If you are heterosexual and you dream that you are having sex with someone of the same sex, signifies not necessarily homosexual desire, but an expression of greater self-love and acceptance. You need to be in better touch with your feminine or masculine side.

To dream that you are the opposite sex suggests that you exhibit or need to incorporate those qualities of the opposite sex. Ask yourself, how do you feel being a man or a woman? In what ways can you incorporate those feelings into your waking life?

Snakes

Snakes are complicated dream symbols and have both positive and negative meanings. To see a snake or be bitten by one in your dream signifies hidden fears and worries that are threatening you. Your dream may be alerting you to something in your waking life that you are not aware of or that has not yet surfaced. The snake may also be seen as phallic and thus symbolize dangerous and forbidden sexuality. The snake may also refer to a person around you who is callous, ruthless, and can't be trusted. As a positive symbol, snakes represent transformation, knowledge, and wisdom. It is indicative of self-renewal and positive changes.

Snakes can also represent primal energy, temptation and evil. These could be the thoughts and feelings you may be trying to suppress. In constantly suppressing your feelings, over time it will overflow to the point where you are forced to confront them.

Fire

Depending on the context of your dream, seeing fire in your dream can symbolize destruction, passion, desire, illumination, transformation, enlightenment, or anger. It may suggest that something old is passing and something new is entering your life. Your thoughts and views are changing. If the fire is under control or contained in one area, it is a metaphor for your internal fire and inner transformation. It also represents your drive and motivation.

To dream that you are being burned by fire indicates that your temper is getting out of control. Some issue or situation is burning you up inside.

To dream that a house is on fire indicates that you need to undergo some transformation. If you have recurring dreams of your family house on fire, then it suggests that you are still not ready for the change or that you are fighting against the change. Alternatively, it highlights the passion and the love of those around you.

To dream that you put out a fire signifies that you will overcome the obstacles in your life through much work and effort.

Trains

To see a train in your dream represents conformity and going along with what everyone else is doing. You need to do things in an orderly and sequential manner. If you see a freight train, then it refers to the burdens and problems that you are hauling around.

To dream that you are on a train is symbolic of your life's journey and suggests that you are on the right track in life and headed in the right direction. Alternatively, you tend to worry needlessly over a situation that will prove to work out in the end.

To see or dream that you are in a train wreck suggests chaos. The path towards achieving your goals is not going according to the way you planned it out. Or you may be lacking self-confidence and doubting your ability to reach your goals.

To dream that you are the engineer signifies that you are in complete control of a particular situation in your waking life. To dream that you miss a train denotes missed opportunities or nearly escaping your death.

Driving

To dream that you are driving a vehicle signifies your life's journey and your path in life. The dream is telling of how you are moving and navigating through life.

If you are driving and cannot see the road ahead of you, then it indicates that you do not know where you are headed in life and what you want to do with yourself. You are lacking direction and goals. If you are driving on a curvy road, then it indicates that you are having difficulties in achieving your goals and the changes associated with them.

To dream that someone else is driving you represents your dependence on the driver. You are not in control of your life and following the goals of others instead of your own. If you are driving from the passenger side of a car, then it suggests that you are trying to gain control of the path that your life is taking. You are beginning to make your own decisions.

To dream that you are driving a cab or bus symbolizes menial labour with few opportunities for advancement.

To dream that you are driving a car in reverse suggests that you are experiencing major setbacks in your goals. If you drive in reverse into a pool of water, then it means that your emotions are holding you back.

To dream that you are driving drunk indicates that your life is out of control. Some relationship or somebody is dominating you.

To dream that you drive off a mountain road suggests that the higher you climb in life, the harder it is to stay at the top. You feel that your advanced position is a precarious one. It takes hard work to remain at the top. You may also feel that you are not able to measure up to the expectations of others.

Seeing a wreck in your dream represents obstacles and barriers toward your goals. You feel that you are being held back or that you are not making any progress.

The car or vehicle itself is supposed to symbolize you in your waking life, in your physical body. Your physical body is used by the soul pretty much like we use a car, it's driven for a while and we give it gas and nourishment and repairs as needed until it stops running, and then we go back home.

Pay attention to your car, which symbolizes your physical body. Are you behind the wheel, or is someone else in control? You want to be in charge of your life, naturally. What is the colour & condition of this vehicle? Do you seem to be driving it the right way, on a safe road in good condition, or is the road rocky, winding, or suddenly ends at a cliff? That would signal you need redirection.

The bigger the vehicle, the more energy you may be successfully using for your daily lessons, depending on the context of your dream. Note all clues as to how you are faring and adjust accordingly.

Ex-Partners

To dream about your ex-boyfriend or girlfriend or ex-husband or wife or that you and your ex got back together again suggests that something or someone in your current life that is bringing out similar feelings you felt during the relationship with your ex.

The dream may be a way of alerting you to the same or similar behaviour in a current relationship. What you learn from that previous relationship may need to be applied to the present one so that you do not repeat the same mistake. Alternatively, past lovers often highlight the positive experiences you had with that person.

To see your ex-husband or wife in your dream indicates that you are finding yourself in a situation that you do not want to be in. It suggests that you are experiencing a similar relationship or situation which makes you feel unhappy and uncomfortable.

To see your mate's ex in your dream suggests that you may be comparing yourself to the ex. The dream is trying to tell you not to make the same relationship mistakes that ended that relationship. Alternatively, seeing your ex in your dream also signifies aspects of yourself that you have crossed out or neglected.

To see an old ex-boyfriend or girlfriend from childhood in your dream refers to a freer, less encumbered relationship. The dream serves to bring you back to a time where the responsibilities of adulthood (or marriage) didn't interfere with the spontaneity of romance. You need to recapture the excitement, freedom, and vitality of youth that is lacking in your present relationship.

To dream that your ex-boyfriend or girlfriend is giving you advice about your current relationship suggests that your subconscious is telling you not to repeat the same mistakes that you had made with this ex.

To dream that you are being massaged by your ex suggests that you need to let go of some of that defensiveness that you have been putting forth. You may have been putting up a wall or armour around you. You need to learn to trust people again.

To dream that your ex gives you a stuffed animal suggests that you are seeking reassuring and nurturing aspects of a relationship. This is not to imply that you want your ex back. Alternatively, the dream could represent some immature relationship that may (or may not) describe the relationship you had with your ex.

To dream that you see your ex dressed in a suit at a hospital suggests that you have come to terms with that relationship and have completed the healing process.

Cheating

To dream that you are cheating on your spouse, mate, fiancé, or significant other suggests feelings of self-guilt and self-betrayal. You may have compromised your beliefs or integrity and/or are wasting your energy and time on fruitless endeavours. Alternatively, it reflects the intensity of sexual passion and exploring areas of your sexuality. It is a reaffirmation of your commitment. Furthermore, it is not uncommon for people approaching a wedding to have dreams about erotic experiences with partners other than their intended spouses. Most likely, such dreams represent the newness of your sexual passion. It may also signify anxieties of changing your identity - that of a spouse.

To dream that your mate, spouse, or significant other is cheating on you indicates your fears of being abandoned.

You may feel a lack of attention in the relationship. Alternatively, you may feel that you are not measuring up to the expectations of others. This notion may stem from issues of trust or self-esteem. The dream could also indicate that you are unconsciously picking up hints and cues that your significant other is not being completely truthful or is not fully committed in the relationship.

To dream that you are cheating at a game suggests that you are not being honest with yourself.

School

This type of dream relates to your current "lesson in life," and if you learn how to interpret it, you'll find out how you are progressing. Think of it as taking a test and getting graded on it!

Our "true selves" are our souls and not our physical bodies. You are a spirit and soul having a physical dream, not the other way around. Ever feel like your life is like a play, and you are acting out some role that you don't even understand, even surprising yourself with your actions sometimes? Bingo!

When we sleep, that proverbial "Veil of Forgetfulness" that prevents us from "cheating on the test" is lifted, and we are shown what type of progress we are making or not making and given guidance on what to do next.

We always have free will in our waking physical lives, though, and if we stubbornly refuse to finish our tests, then we have that right – but we are doomed to repeat it until we pass it, and each time we turn away from it, the next time it will be more unpleasant until finally we are forced to acknowledge its importance for our growth.

The things we consider vitally important in our waking physical lives are not nearly as important as the TRUE reason we are here, which is to overcome our shortcomings so that we may get closer to our Source/God/Higher Power. Don't avoid learning the lesson or you will find yourself repeating the same tasks repeatedly never making any progress.

A House

Dreams about a house symbolize a larger aspect of yourself and the aspects of self that make the whole. Each room is said to symbolize a different aspect of yourself, for example:

An ATTIC symbolizes your Higher Self, and your spiritual development & progress. Look at other symbols in the attic of your dream and try to evaluate what they mean. Also, pay attention to the *feeling* you experience in your dream...is it pensive, enlightening or what, exactly? All these things are clues for you.

A BATHROOM would symbolize the need for cleansing/purging/elimination of something in your life that isn't quite working or that has served its purpose and now it's time to move on.

A KITCHEN would symbolize the need or act of supplying nourishment or food for the body/mind/soul...whatever is currently "cooking" or developing in your life. If the food is plentiful, you have what you need. If the cupboard is bare, time to go shopping for new nourishment, and you need to figure out what is needed for that "shopping list."

A DINING ROOM is like the kitchen but has more to do with immediate needs for supplying & utilizing nourishment, and less with the preparation or taking stock of those needs.

THE MAIN ROOM or LIVING ROOM symbolizes your daily interactions with others, and often you will have other people appearing in your dreams in this room.

Remember, they represent aspects of yourself, and not themselves. (See PEOPLE, above)

BEDROOMS symbolize the unconscious mind aspect of yourself, rest, dreams, and sometimes, sexuality issues in your life.

THE UPSTAIRS symbolizes your spiritual awareness aspect of self, or the Higher Self that holds all the keys or knowledge to this life's role you are acting out, and always have your higher good looked after, no matter how it might seem otherwise.

THE DOWNSTAIRS/BASEMENT symbolizes your subconscious mind aspect of self, which deals with habits, old coping skills, automation, and ego. That's usually the part of ourselves that makes us feel "torn" between knowing we should do one thing, and inexplicably ending up doing the opposite. Old belief patterns & fears must be corrected if that is the case. Tackle & overcome it, and you will feel much more peaceful about your life.

THE GROUND FLOOR of a house represents your daily agenda; what's currently going on in your life.

REVISITING OLD HOUSES FROM CHILDHOOD OR EARLIER TIMES: This points to issues that probably are resurfacing in your current life, and need to be looked at, analyzed, and healed so you can move forward and not look back. If you find yourself repeating the same old tired mistakes, or dealing with the same old tired fears, chances are you will have this dream.

A HALLWAY symbolizes that you have reached an area that is necessary to journey through to get to the other side, and it may be a narrow path that has to be traversed with care and awareness. If you have that "closed in, claustrophobic feeling" then you need to expand your awareness and open your mind to more possibilities for completing this phase of your journey.

A PORCH symbolizes perhaps a metaphor of being undecided, such as the saying, "I'm still on the porch on that decision." It could be symbolic of being contemplative, or uncommitted or withdrawn. It could be something entirely different such as being on the threshold of a new sense or an extension of self. It depends on the entire context of the dream. Is it the back or front porch? Is it screened-in or open, messy, or neat, sparse, or furnished? All these details add to the overall symbolism.

Colours

Experts believe that almost everyone dreams in colour. If a major portion of your dream reflects a consistent colour theme, this could have some type of meaning in interpreting that dream. Below are the major colours and what they could mean.

Black

Black symbolizes the unknown, unconscious, danger, mystery, darkness, death, mourning, hate or malice. If the feeling in the dream is one of joy, blackness could imply hidden spirituality and divine qualities.

To dream in black and white suggests that you need to be more objective in formulating your decisions. You may be a little too unyielding in your thought process and thus need to find some sort of balance between two opposing views. Consider the views and opinions of others. Alternatively, black, and white dreams are signs of depression or sadness. You may feel that there is not enough excitement in your life.

Blue

Blue represents truth, wisdom, heaven, eternity, devotion, tranquillity, loyalty, and openness. The presence of this colour in your dream may symbolize your spiritual guide and your optimism about the future. You have clarity of mind. Depending on the context of your dream, the colour blue may also be a metaphor for "being blue" and feeling sad

Brown

Brown denotes worldliness, practicality, domestic and physical comfort, conservatism, and a materialistic character. Brown also represents the ground and earth.

Gold

The golden colour reflects your spiritual rewards, richness, refinement, and enhancement of your surroundings.

Green

Green signifies a positive change, good health, growth, healing, hope, vigour, vitality, peace, and serenity. Green is also symbolic of your strive to gain recognition and establish your independence. Money, wealth, and jealousy are often associated with this colour. Dark green indicates materialism, cheating, deceit, or difficulties with sharing. You need to balance between your masculine and feminine attributes.

Gray

Gray indicates fear, fright, depression, ill health, ambivalence, and confusion. You may feel emotionally distant or detached.

Orange

Orange denotes friendliness, courtesy, lively, sociability, and an out-going nature. You may want to expand your horizons and look into new interests.

Pink

Pink represents love, joy, sweetness, happiness, affection, kindness. Being in love or healing through love is also implied with this colour.

Purple

Purple is indicative of devotion, healing abilities, loving, kindness, and compassion. It is also the colour of royalty, high rank, and dignity.

Red

Red is an indication of raw energy, force, vigour, intense passion, aggression, power, courage, and passion. The colour red has deep emotional and spiritual connotations. Red is also the colour of danger, shame, sexual impulses, and urges. Perhaps you need to stop and think about your actions.

White

White represents purity, perfection, peace, innocence, dignity, cleanliness, awareness, and new beginnings. You may be experiencing a reawakening or have a fresh outlook on life. However, in Eastern cultures, white is associated with death and mourning

Yellow

The colour yellow has both positive and negative connotations. If the dream is a pleasant one, then the colour yellow is symbolic of intellect, energy, agility, happiness, harmony, and wisdom.

On the other hand, if the dream is an unpleasant one, then the colour represents cowardice and sickness. You may have a fear or an inability to decide or act. As a result, you are experiencing many setbacks.

Death

To dream about the death of a loved one suggests that you are lacking a certain aspect or quality that the loved one embodies. Ask yourself what makes this person special or what do you like about him. It is that very quality that you are lacking in your relationship or circumstances. Alternatively, it indicates that whatever that person represents has no part in your own life.

To dream that you die in your dream, symbolizes inner changes, transformation, self-discovery, and positive development that is happening within you or in your life.

Although such dreams may bring about feelings of fear and anxiety, it is not cause for alarm and is often considered a positive symbol. Dreams of experiencing your death usually mean that big changes are ahead for you. They mean you are moving on to new beginnings and leaving the past behind.

These changes do not necessarily imply a negative turn of events. Metaphorically, dying can be seen as an end or a termination of your old ways and habits. So, dying does not always mean physical death, but an ending of something.

On a negative note, to dream that you die may represent involvement in deeply painful relationships or unhealthy, destructive behaviours. You may feel depressed or feel strangled by a situation or person in your waking life. Perhaps your mind is preoccupied with someone who is terminally ill or dying. Alternatively, you may be trying to get out of some obligation, responsibility, or other situation.

To see someone dying in your dream signifies that your feelings for that person are dead or that a significant change or loss is occurring in your relationship with that person. Alternatively, you may want to repress that aspect of yourself that is represented by the dying person.

Love and Lust

To dream of being in love suggests intense feelings carried over from a waking relationship. It implies happiness and contentment with what you have and where you are in life. On the other hand, you may not be getting enough love in your daily life. We naturally long for the sense to belong and to be accepted.

To see a couple in love or expressing love to each other, indicates much success ahead for you.

To dream that your friend is in love with you may be one of wish fulfilment. Perhaps you have developed feelings for your best friend and are wondering how he or she feels. You are so preoccupied with these thoughts that it is evitable that it finds its way into your dreaming mind.

On the other hand, the dream may also suggest that you have accepted certain qualities of your best friend and incorporated them into your character.

To dream that you are making love in public or different places relates to some overt sexual issue or need. Your dream may be telling you that you need to express yourself more openly. Alternatively, it represents your perceptions about your sexuality in the context of political and social norms. You may be questioning your feelings about sex, marriage, love, and gender roles.

To dream of lust, suggests that you are lacking or feeling unfulfilled in some aspect of your life. Alternatively, you need to exercise some self-control.

Aliens

To dream that you are an alien symbolizes the undiscovered part of yourself. Your manifestation as an alien may be your way of 'escaping' from reality. Dreams of this nature also symbolize your outlandish ideas and your wild imagination.

To dream that you are being abducted by aliens indicates your fears of your changing surroundings or your fear of losing your home and family. You feel that your space and/or privacy is being invaded.

To see aliens in your dream signifies that you are having difficulties adapting and adjusting to your new surroundings. You are feeling "alienated" and invaded. On a psychological level, seeing aliens may represent an encounter with an unfamiliar or neglected aspect of yourself.

Angels

To see angels in your dream signifies an unusual disturbance in your soul. Angels symbolize goodness, purity, and protection and comfort and consolation. Pay careful attention to the message that the angels are trying to convey. These messages serve as a guide toward greater fulfilment and happiness. Angels may appear in your dream because of your wicked and mean-hearted activities.

To see an angel holding a scroll in your dream indicates a highly spiritual dream. Your future and goals are clearer to you in dreams of this type. The message on the scroll is particularly significant.

Children

To see children in your dream signifies your childlike qualities or a retreat to a childlike state. It is an extension of your inner child during a time of innocence, purity, simplicity, and a carefree attitude. You may be longing for the past and the chance to satisfy repressed desires and unfulfilled hopes. Take some time off and cater to the inner child within. Perhaps there is something that you need to see grow and nurture.

To dream that your grown children are still very young indicates that you still see them as young and dependent. You want to feel needed and significant.

To dream that you are watching children, but they do not know you are there is a metaphor for some hidden knowledge or some latent talent that you have failed to recognize. To save a child signifies your attempts to save a part of yourself from being destroyed.

Dead People

To see the dead in your dream forewarns that you are being influenced by negative people and are hanging around the wrong crowd. You may suffer material loss. This dream may also be a way for you to resolve your feelings with those who have passed on.

To see and talk with your dead father in your dream signifies that you are about to enter into an unlucky transaction or rotten deal. Thoroughly think through your decisions before entering into them.

To see your dead mother in your dream signifies your wretched and mean-hearted nature towards others around you. Seeing your dead parents in your dreams may mean your fears of losing them or your way of coping with the loss. You may want that last opportunity to say your final goodbyes to them.

To see your dead sibling, relative, or friend in your dream foretells that you will soon be called on for aid and assistance. It may also mean that you miss them and are trying to relive the old experiences you had with them. In trying to keep up with the pace of your daily waking life, your dreams may serve as your only outlet in coping and coming to terms with the loss of a loved one.

Do not fear conversation with the so-called "dead" in dreams. If the communication is one-sided, it denotes telepathy. If both participate, it may be an actual encounter of a bodiless consciousness.

Accidents

To dream that you are in an accident signifies pent up guilt and you are subconsciously punishing yourself over it.

To dream of a car accident symbolizes your emotional state. You may be harbouring deep anxieties and fears. Are you "driving" yourself too hard? This dream may tell you to slow down before you hit disaster. You need to rethink or re-plan your course of action and set yourself on a better path.

To dream that a loved one dies in an accident indicates that something in yourself that is no longer functional and is "dead". It is also symbolic of your relationship with that person. Perhaps you need to let go of this relationship.

Accident dreams may also represent your straightforward fears of being an actual, physical accident. You may be simply nervous about getting behind the wheel. This dream may be a clear warning to be cautious of approaching vehicles.

This is only a general partial list – of course. Every single detail in your dream could have some hidden meaning. There are a lot of places online to find information about the specific details of your dreams and what they might mean.

You need to discover the link between all these images and what they might mean. This process is a bit like those “connect the dots” puzzles that reveal a hidden picture. Psychologically, you simply need to understand what this net of associations from the dream is telling you specifically, at this precise time of your life, about your current problems and conflicts.

Quite often, these associations are purely emotional; that is, you can take a particularly graphic dream image, examine your emotional reactions to it, look back into your past for times when you felt the same emotions, and then ask yourself in what way those situations from the past have any bearing on what is happening in your life now

Repetitive dreams indicate that you are continuing to miss the point about the meaning of the dream. If you don’t “wake up” to the unconscious meaning of the dream but instead persist in seeing it through your own wish-fulfilment needs, you will remain stuck in your self-deception.

Almost everyone has experienced a nightmare at one point or time in their life.

CHAPTER SIX

Nightmares

Children, especially, are prone to nightmares. Nightmares are common in children, typically beginning at around age three and occurring up to age seven to eight. People with an anxiety disorder might also experience what experts term "night terrors". These are panic attacks that occur in sleep. It is especially difficult to remember these types of dreams since they conjure up terrifying images that we would just as soon forget.

In poetic myth, the Nightmare is a "small nettlesome mare, not more than thirteen hands high, of the breed familiar with the Elgin marbles: cream-coloured, clean-limbed, with a long head, bluish eye, flowing mane and tail." Her nests, called mares' nests, "when one comes across them in dreams, lodged in rock-clefs or the branches of enormous hollow yews, are built of carefully chosen twigs lined with white horse-hair and the plumage of prophetic birds and littered with the jaw-bones and entrails of poets."

Thus, in a pagan world of myth and blood sacrifice, the Nightmare was a cruel, fearful creature. Our modern word *nightmare* derives from the Middle English *nihtmare* (from *niht*, night, and *mare*, demon), an evil spirit believed to haunt and suffocate sleeping people. And so, in today's world, when we speak of a nightmare, we mean a frightening dream accompanied by a sensation of oppression and helplessness.

The blood-thirsty aspect of the mythic Nightmare, however, can give a good clue about nightmares in general, for in psychodynamic terms nightmares are graphic depictions of raw, primitive emotions such as aggression and rage that have not been incorporated into the conscious psyche. Thus, we tend to encounter these "ugly" aspects of our unconscious lives as terrifying dream images in whose presence we feel completely helpless.

Nightmares are quite common in childhood because this is a time of our emotional development when we all must come to terms with, well, raw, primitive emotions such as aggression and rage.

Traumatic nightmares can also occur as one of the many symptoms of posttraumatic stress disorder (PTSD). Repetitive, intrusive nightmares following a trauma often contain symbolic themes that mirror the original trauma and relate to the threat to life, the threat of abandonment or death, or loss of identity.

Therefore, traumatic nightmares need to be treated differently than other dreams. It's not enough just to "know" intellectually the psychological reasons why you have these nightmares. An event is traumatic because it disrupts your previously secure (and illusory) sense of "self." And so, to heal from a trauma, you must take the initiative to make conscious changes in your life to accommodate the traumatic shattering of your illusions about life and identity.

Some believe that nightmares have a physiological nature as well. Edgar Cayce believed that Nightmares, which bring with them an inability to move or cry out, usually indicate the wrong diet. To end the nightmarish dreams, change your diet.

We found a technique online that can help people who suffer from recurrent nightmares. It is not meant to be a cure-all. It is just a suggested treatment to deal with frightening nightmares. The idea is to use this therapy every night until the nightmare has been resolved. It is called Imagery Rehearsal Therapy.

Here are the steps of Imagery Rehearsal Therapy:

Write out the text of the nightmare. Tell the story, no matter how frightening, in as much detail as you can remember. Create a new ending for the nightmare story and write it out. Be careful, however, to make the new ending peaceful. Remember that the nightmare is grounded in emotions such as raw anger that has been provoked by a trauma. The point of a new ending is to "tame" the emotions, not merely vent them in violence and revenge.

Rehearse the new version of the story in your imagination each night just before going to sleep. Do this as close as possible to your falling asleep without any other activity between the rehearsal and sleep.

Perform a relaxation exercise. Do this immediately after the rehearsal to fall asleep peacefully. You may use any technique with which you are familiar. This could be meditation, yoga, or breathing exercises. The "cousin" of nightmares is disturbing dreams with unpleasant images.

Disturbing Dreams

Disturbing dreams aren't quite nightmares. They may cause you to wonder what exactly your subconscious is trying to tell you.

First, the dreams could be unconscious advice. Maybe in some way you are betraying yourself, forgetting something, or not fulfilling your potential. For example, persons on the edge of a midlife career change may have dreams about being in school and searching for a missing classroom, or they may find themselves in a class about to take a final exam while realizing that they completely forgot to attend the class all year. The feeling of panic in the dream points to the real feeling of panic in their current life about the failure of their present career.

Second, the dreams could be an admonition, based on guilt. Imagine, for example, that you are embezzling the bank for which you work. Then you start having dreams about burglars breaking into your home.

Well, the dreams are simply a depiction of something happening to you that is like the hurt or moral injury you are inflicting on someone else. This same dynamic often occurs in children's nightmares: in waking life, children often experience angry feelings toward their parents and yet lack the cognitive capacity to express these feelings openly; so, in unconscious guilt, the anger becomes turned against themselves as a threatening nightmare images.

Third, the dreams could be hints of repressed trauma. As I say above, nightmares often accompany the emotional pain of a traumatic event experienced in adulthood. But if trauma in childhood is repressed, dreams reflecting the emotional intensity of the trauma can persist throughout life – as a repetition compulsion – until the trauma is eventually brought to conscious awareness and healed.

Finally, the dreams could be psychic premonitions. This is a rare phenomenon, but it does happen to some persons.

The best advice we've found about disturbing dreams is to just ignore them. You can try to analyze the images you find, but that is most likely not going to give you the answers you need.

Conclusion

Dream analysis and interpretation isn't the mystical science that it seems to be. It's simply remembering your dreams and then figuring out what your subconscious is trying to tell you about your life and anything that might be happening in your life.

You should keep in mind that dream analysis is simply an interpretation of your dreams, not a definitive answer for all that "ails" you, so to speak.

If you are having some major life problems, we suggest you seek the assistance of a trained professional. You can still, however, pay close attention to your dreams and report them to your therapist for some insight into your troubles.

Your dreams are unique to you. They can represent all that is good in you and all that you need to improve upon. When you better understand your dreams, you can better understand yourself. Sleep well!

References

The following websites were used in researching this book:

www.dreammoods.com
www.wiki.ehow.com
www.dreamemporium.com
www.near-death.com
www.about.com

9 798885 213981

Printed by Libri Plureos GmbH in Hamburg, Germany